The Path to Positive INTERNAL Power

HOW TO BUILD SELF-ESTEEM IN CHILDREN AND ADULTS

"Instruct a wise man and he will be wiser still."
~ Proverbs 9:9

Dr. Ray W. Lincoln

Studies in Biblical Psychology

ISBN: 978-0-9996349-1-2
LCCN: 2019901199

Contents

The Path to Positive INTERNAL Power   1

Getting Understanding   1

    PART ONE   11

How Is Self-Image or Self-Belief Developed?   11

    PART TWO   19

How Do We Change Our Self-Image?   19

The Path to Positive Internal Power   23

    PART THREE   39

Helping Our Children to a Strong Self-Image   39

Understand Your Child and How He/She Feels   47

    PART FOUR   51

Helping Teenagers to Self-Image Power   51

Conclusion   55

Dedication

I've spent some soul-searching moments trying to remember who took time to help me build my self-worth. Most of my memories are about people who rammed home to me how contaminated I was with the sin of the human race and how I have added to the messy pile of debris with my own efforts.

I don't deny this, but it is a very depressing thought. No one could say thinking that way builds self-esteem. It certainly alerts us to the damage inflicted by our wayward actions and non-actions and it brings us in touch with our sinful reality. This we must realize. But is it the only way we are to be thinking of ourselves? Is it the dominant thought pattern that we should carry around with us?

One person stands out above all others. Perhaps it is because she is the only one with whom I have shared my inner self. I have a feeling it is more so because she loves me even though she knows my shortcomings. I mean really loves me. My inner fire has been lit by merely typing those words!

What an incalculable blessing it is to have a person who be-lieves in you and loves you! Feelings of self-worth grow best in the fertile soil of love. Although this book is about how you can build your own self-esteem, I want you to be aware of what can be done for you by others. Simply put, you are well aided in the quest of self-esteem if you are loved and appreci-ated lots. My thanks to my wife and lover, Mary Jo.

Getting Understanding

"Though it cost all you have get understanding." ~Proverbs 4:7.

What a tremendous need there is for believing in ourselves up to the full measure of faith God has given us (Romans 12:3). We can't go far in this world until we know ourselves so we need to know what that level is. Have we tried to make an honest assessment of ourselves? What is the level of belief God requires of us and, for that matter, has in us?

To agree with God's assessment of us is to step into the love and grace of God who thinks we are wonderful. He created us and sent His Son to die for us; and He wouldn't do either for useless, worthless beings. God's assessment of us is the best place for our belief about ourselves to begin. This fact is the basis for the method that I have devised for the improvement of our self-images.

Many have come to me and indignantly reminded me of the words of Jesus to the man who called Him "good Teacher". Jesus said, "Why do you call me good? No one is good except God above." " You see," they say, "Jesus tells us plainly we are NOT good!"

Oh, really? Then why did He contradict His Father, God, who said we are very good (Genesis 1:31)? It should be clear after a little thought that the meaning of the word is different in the two places. In Genesis 1:31 God looks at His magnificent creation with its climactic act of fashioning a human in His own image and declares it is all very good. Something made by God in His own image, by necessity, must be very, very good! That's the sense in which I use the word good of each of us. Jesus explains His own use of the word *good* in Mark 10:18 when He goes on to ask if the man has kept all of God's laws. He was asking, "Are you perfect? Have you kept all God's command-ments?" And the answer for all of us is, of course, "No."

Are we perfect? No. Are we very good? Yes. Our failures don't erase God's good work in creating us. "We are fearfully and wonderfully made." (Psalm 139:14)

To form a workable partnership with God means to believe in God and ourselves as He believes in us. We can then become effective partners in God's work in us and in our world.

Perhaps we should recall some of what God thinks of us. He says:
1. We are the salt of the earth. (Matthew 5:13)
2. We are the light of the world. (Matthew 5:14)
3. We are sons and daughters of God. (John 1:12)
4. We are very good. (Genesis 1:31)
5. If we believe, we can do the impossible. (Mark 9:23; Matthew 17:20) That's believing in us!
6. We are His chosen home base in this world. (I Corinthians 3:17)
7. The Holy Spirit makes us His temple, a place where God is worshipped. (I Corinthians 3:17)

8. And above all, God loves us and always will. Jesus was willing to die for us! That's believing in us!

I can't enter into a partnership with God unless I respect and believe what He says. I cannot select what I want to believe from all that God has said and trash the rest, either. That's saying I'll be the judge of when God is right or wrong. Wow! That's presumptuous and a sure way to nullify the effectiveness of the partnership.

To be propelled by a positive internal power is to benefit from a healthy self-esteem that motivates and drives your personal engine. Do you want to feel energized and confident in your attempts to succeed in whatever you know is God's will for you? Then your self-esteem needs all the fuel it can get. Self-esteem is not some unreal entity dreamed up by psychologists to wile away their time and accommodate their desire for obscure, ethereal concepts. It is a very real part of us. A self-conscious being, by definition, has a self-image. God gave it to us when he created us in His image. God has one too!

I find it so inspiring to watch a person's self-image develop — like Pat for instance, who came to me because he was sick of his self-pity. He had little going for him and he had little to lose so he poured his efforts into doing whatever he could to improve his faith in God and his belief in himself. He told me it felt good to say to himself that God loved him and to say he could be what he and God had planned for him to be. But his self-pitying attitudes had massaged his mind into accepting his feelings of worthlessness as excuses, and he had grown tired of this false comfort. Why was he spending his life convincing himself that he had no future and that he wasn't very good?

Excuses, he was learning, got him nowhere. His dream was slipping away. With a little coaching the starved urge to be someone soon grew to mammoth proportions and he became obsessed with hope instead of hopelessness. Determination followed and, finally, after several set backs (which we can all expect) he started his training for a pilot's license. The dream was on its way. His faith in the words "I can do all things through Christ who strengthens me" gave him a new vision of life. Faith in God was what powered his ability to believe in himself. If God loved him with all his perceived failings and his feelings of guilt, he figured he could come to terms with the discrepancy between what God felt about him and what he felt about himself and believe what God believed about him. A healthy mind is one that solves these discrepancies of belief and finds harmony. Will he succeed all the way to his dream? Make your guess. I've made mine!

Without a belief in ourselves we do little and become nothing. God believes in us. When we don't believe in ourselves, we fail to live up to the image in which we are created: His image. We also offend Him since we do not agree with His valuation of us. Into the bargain we look weak and purposeless — wimpy losers. And self-image, in case you are wondering, is nothing but a title for all the beliefs we have about ourselves.

A surgeon can't find those beliefs, cut them open and repair them. They exist in our mind, and our mind is not surgical material. The only way to lastingly repair it or strengthen our self-image is through the changes we make in our own minds, and that, too, is the journey I am about to show you. God put the repair mechanism in your system and you are the only one who can activate it.

Now, for its power. Without a belief, we do nothing. We don't eat unless we believe several things: the food is safe to eat; it looks appetizing; we feel hungry; and so on. So what we believe holds the ultimate power over us. It controls all we do. What we believe about ourselves determines what we will attempt to do and what we won't attempt to do. It defines our confidence level and our determination. An athlete knows that it determines what he/she can and can't accomplish. It determines so much that we could fill several pages with the items it controls and then not mention them all. Its power over us is total, so you can be very certain of one thing: God wants us to have strong self-images.

Having a strong self-image is having a strong faith in both sides of the partnership you formed when you began following Christ - a faith in God and in yourself. Our self-esteem is strongest when we have an unwavering faith in God and ourselves — both! We lose essential power when we fail to believe in either partner.

5

Imagine trying to set up a partnership with God with these words:

> Lord, I believe in you. That's why I want you to be my partner; but I don't believe in myself. That won't matter will it — even if you believe in me? Or will it matter? Will you establish a partnership with me if I don't agree with your idea of my own worth? I don't mean to say that you are wrong, of course. Do your words, "Have faith in God," really mean I have to believe all that you say and believe?

Could we get away with that?

We cannot outperform our self-image (our belief about ourselves) and that is front page news. Low self-image equals low performance in all things. Don't contaminate your mind with the lie that this is true only for the physical side of your life. It's for the spiritual part of us and for our whole lives. Can you imagine a disciple of Jesus offering their life as a living sacrifice to God with these words:

> It's not much, Lord, but I want to give to you, this pitiful shell of a person that I am, so that you can use me. I don't believe I'm much, In fact I'm nothing; yes, less than nothing; and I can't imagine why you ever gave your life for me or made me in the first place. Accept this useless piece of clay, Amen.

I was taught to pray that kind of disparaging prayer when I was young — and I did! I've long since apologized to God for such a pathetic offering. But for years, the feeling of total worth-lessness (which was thought to be the ultimate in holiness by some misguided Bible teachers) has haunted my spirit and played havoc with my commitment to God. Thank God a million times that I came to say with Paul, "I (yes, I – that's me!) can do all things with Christ…" To say that and believe it is to discover how it feels to be accepted into the world's greatest partnership scheme and be invited to perform at your highest level. Nothing is any longer impossible. The words of Jesus, "Everything is possible to the one who believes," (Mark 9:23) fill us with new energy when we can believe them! When we do believe them God's image in us is not in conflict with our image of ourselves. Let's say these words again together: "Everything is possible to the one who believes." A partnership with God deserves that I be all that I can be; and I can't if I don't believe in myself!

Most people — in fact, I would say all — need a stronger self-image. Are you one of those whose self-esteem is dragging its chin on the gravel? Are you down on yourself, talking dirty to the one God loves? Do you long to be confident and dream to be someone, but seem to constantly fail and back out of the fight because you are overcome with fears that hinder you from achieving your goals and desires? THEN, READ ON! THIS IS FOR YOU! Yes, I mean this booklet will turn your life around and power you toward being the best that you can be. Again, is that what you want? God wants it for you!

What Is Self-Concept?

Self-concept, self-esteem, self-image, or self-worth are synonyms for our purpose. Although they don't mean exactly the same, they refer to the same idea: what we believe about ourselves.

Self-concept is:
• What we think, feel and believe about ourselves.
• The <u>way</u> we think, feel and believe about ourselves.

Whatever thoughts you have about yourself form an atmosphere in which your mind operates for good or ill. All our thoughts are affected by this 'air' that our mind breathes. A healthy mind must have lots of positive self-belief to operate to its designer's standards.

Now, I know you want to feel the internal peace and the high voltage charge of loving yourself and feeling good about yourself. Let's walk the path to feeling even better than you feel about yourself right now and, at the same time, increase your belief in God. Sound good? The two must go together to maximize our possibilities.

We will first learn about self-image in adults, how it is developed and how to change it. Then it will be easy to relate how adults can help children and partner with teenagers to empower them.

I will attempt to present the following instructions in the form of an outline so as to maintain brevity and make for quick reference. After all, the goal of this book is to give you a workbook format for learning how to change your self-image.

10

PART ONE

How Is Self-Image or Self-Belief Developed?

1. Some believe we are born with no self-image, with a blank disc, and that we start writing on it from birth. I think this is unlikely. Some kind of self-esteem seems essential to life for a self-conscious being. A self-conscious being thinks and feels things about itself; and that, in essence, is a self-image.

2. Others believe we are born with a healthy self-image — normal, if you like. I think this makes sense. As we grow we mold our self-image. Positive or negative factors elevate it or shrink it.

3. *All 'events' — meaning every happening, from the comments and behavior of others, to circumstances, plus our own actions and reactions — are labeled by us as good or bad. The labeling is what molds our self-images.*

   A. *Examples: (1) We do something bad and know it to be against our own feelings and beliefs and the result is we damage our self-esteem by destroying our inner integrity. It results in what we call guilt. (2) We are called "useless" or an "idiot" by someone and we affirm the comment to ourselves. Again, we damage our self-esteem. This is called putting ourselves down or self-degradation. (3) We reject the bad comment about us made by someone else, believ-*

11

ing instead that God loves us, and a lift to our self-esteem is the result. Our belief makes the difference.

B. **These events can be external or internal.** *EX-TERNAL means all things that happen outside of ourselves. INTERNAL means all things that happen inside of ourselves. All self-talk (psycholinguistics) is an event inside ourselves — the most potent of events that shape our self-image, as we shall see.*

C. **We label all events (external or internal) as "accepted" or "rejected"** *and they are stored in our memory banks (sub-conscious) building our self-image and remaining there ready to be recalled for evidence when needed. (Our own health threatening statements like, "The evidence is clear: I always mess things up," come out of the trash we have labeled "accepted" and stored.)*

4. **It's our responses to the events, not the events themselves, that lift or lower our self-image. Our responses (beliefs about them) are our way of labeling them.**

A. I often hear people blaming their mother for their beliefs about themselves. But what their mother did to them did not affect their self-image. How they responded to what their mother did or said is what formed their self-image. We MUST understand this clearly or we will never be able to effectively change our self-images. We will always blame others and then their control over us continues.

12

It's like Tom who went on vacation to a tropical paradise. He felt he needed the break because his boss had by-passed him for a promotion and the sting of this perceived injustice angered him. He took his anger with him on the vacation and it haunted his every effort to relax. Blaming his boss soured his meals and interrupted his sleep. He was letting his boss control him, even though he was hundreds of miles away.

B. *I can't even blame my circumstances for my self-image!* I must realize, likewise, that it is my response to my circumstances that creates my self-image.

C. *Neither should I blame or condemn myself for my self-image!* Only God has the right to condemn exact punishment — "It is mine to avenge; I will repay," Deuteronomy 32:35. I simply accept the responsibility for what I have done to my self-image. Blame? Condemn? Never!

Responsibility means I admit that I did it; condemnation means I condemn myself for what I did. An admission that we did wrong does not damage our human spirits. In fact, it confirms the integrity of our human spirit. But condemning ourselves ruins our confidence and turns our belief about ourselves negative, adding all the resultant damage to our psyches.

Romans 8:1 tells us that God has even given up His right to condemn people who are living by His Spirit. "There is therefore, now, no condemnation for those who are in Christ Jesus... who live not according to the flesh but according to the Spirit." These are the people who live like God lives, filling themselves with love, joy and peace — the fruit of God's Spirit at work in them. They take responsibility for all they do and can rest contentedly in the knowledge that not even God condemns them. Therefore, they don't accept the condemnation of others for their mistakes, either. They are positive through and through. THIS IS THE ULTIMATE WAY TO LIVE – with the ultimate healthy self-image. Attaining this positive ability to reject the hurtful criticisms of others is what I want you to learn.

D. ***It may surprise you to read that I am happy to take responsibility for my choices,*** and I do so because that gives me the opportunity to change what I have done. If others must take the responsibility for my failures or rotten self-image. I can't do anything to change my sad state because I am not responsible, and I can't change other people! I'm stuck with who I am. That's the worst thing that could happen to a person with a low self-image. And yet, that is what they persistently trot out as their belief. "My mother made me the way I am," or "my circumstances are responsible for my thoughts about myself!" Now they are trapped and must accept their self-made fate.

5. ***Every time another similar event occurs*** (<u>Example</u>: we are called an "idiot" by someone else) our memory files the new event with all the other similar entries and we compare them. This comparing is often only a matter of running them by our feelings, not through a logical thinking process. Then we label the new event according to our current feeling about ourselves, either strengthening or weakening our self-image. We have thousands of these events stored and labeled in our memories.

6. ***Thousands of events have created a persona*** (a public psyche or image, if you like) — an image that we unconsciously or consciously show the world. This public self-image has been built up over all our years.

Sheldon was born into an average family. There was enough food to go around and he developed both physically and spiritually. However, his mother's temper broke the charm of those early years. She exploded in a white-hot rage whenever he failed to meet her expectations. He withered under each blast and told himself that he must be less than okay since he failed his mother so often.

His father was consumed with making more money to ease their situation and provide for his golf passions. He was gentle but absent, and when at home, remote, having no time to show love, but thinking he was simply doing his best. Sheldon was also hurt by this passive rejection that he felt from his father and again took the blame on him-

*self for not being good enough to attract his father's love
(labeling himself "no good").*

*Once he made a desperate but ill-conceived approach to a
girl for her affection and she shunned him, saying, "I
wouldn't go out with you if you were the last nerd in town."
Failed exams, introverted shyness, and a teacher's impa-
tience led to more derogatory self-talk, and he arrived for
help in my office with a self-image sprinting for cover.
These were the low points in hundreds of days of feeling
worthless and inferior to his peers. The non-dramatic days
were as critical as the notably destructive days in whipping
his self-image into despair. Sheldon was a dark shadow of
condemned humanity and the world told him so. He believed what it told him, too. His public image reflected all
the above.*

7. **The world reacts to this persona.** If it is an angry
persona that the world sees, the world returns anger or
an appropriate response. It feeds back to us according to
what we show it of ourselves. That's why Proverbs advises
us to change the way other people react to us by changing
the way we act to them. For example, it says, "A soft answer turns away wrath," Proverbs 15:1. Paul puts it this
way, "Whatever we sow we reap," Galatians 6:7. The Bible
is full of reminders like this to change ourselves so that we
can change the way the world sees us and reacts to us!
So, the truth is we can change our world by changing what
we believe about ourselves. We exude the odor of our

self-image wherever we go. A person with a poor self-image seeking a job is spotted for what they are and given a non-responsible job. Had they shown a confident self-image, the job they received would most likely have been a better job and they would probably have sought a better job in the first place. The world doesn't owe us a good living. We are the ones who prod it to respond to us the way it does. We owe ourselves a winning self-image. That's all we need to better our place in life. If we believe in ourselves we make our partnership with God a winning partnership, too.

8. *However the world treats you it is a confirmation of your beliefs about yourself.* We have just said the world gives us feedback. Now, we must remember that the world's feedback is always reliable. It will tell us how good it believes we are based on what we have shown it. I said above that I am glad I must take responsibility for what I do. And I am also glad the world gives me this reliable feedback. Otherwise, I would not know how the world hears me and, therefore, what I am projecting to the world.

   A. Remember how God designed life to work? "Whatever a person sows, they will reap."

   B. At harvest time the wise learn a lesson and sow no more bad seeds. The foolish sow what they reap. **They replant with the same bad seeds!** How often have we done this? Our poor self-image is lowered further by what we have foolishly replanted.

9. *Prayer is also a means of getting feedback.* This is how prayer gives feedback. Tell God what you really be-

17

lieve about yourself (<u>Example:</u> I believe I will never be anything worthwhile) and ask him to let you know if it is the same as his belief about you. You should receive a loud "No!" which could be registered in your mind by a feeling of uneasiness or the simple conviction that you have lied.

The history of our self-images is **our** history. We can't avoid the conclusion that we are the culprit or benefactor. No one can make changes to it except us. Let's find how to make those changes.

PART TWO

How Do We Change Our Self-Image?

"Happy is the man who finds wisdom and gains understanding,"
Proverbs 3:13.

All of us determine our own value.
We are made useless or useful, small or great, by our own consent.

A personality assessment (PA) is a big help in finding out how God made us so that we can use that knowledge to our advantage. (For a child's PA we need the parent's help to define how the child behaves, since the child has not enough experiences or understanding to define its choices.) If you haven't had a personality assessment with an interpretation based in Biblical Psychology, think hard about getting one now. Without a personality assessment we can still change our self-image and that of our children, but with more difficulty and less effectively. Without one, I find most parents shooting in the dark as to what is the best way to help their children and as to how their children feel when they act or refuse to act.

Our self-image is made up of known and unknown causes — things that we can recall and things we can't easily recall — that have damaged or positively built our self-worth. No matter! Those thousands of responses we can't recall don't need to be recalled. If they did we would never repair the damage

19

we have done to ourselves. Only divine surgery on our mind and spirit could rescue us and God won't perform emergency surgery when he has written into our makeup a way to do the same thing with the conscious involvement of our faith.

It may be depressing to realize that every event known or unknown to us in our past has contributed to our current self-image. That is true. But all it takes to reverse the damage is to build a new mental path. The Bible calls it "renewing your mind" (Romans 12:2). We cannot be the best we were created to be unless we learn to think like God thinks. Just like one brief determining moment in our past changed us for good or ill, so a brief period of correction can change our self-image in the present. How long it will take depends on us.

Marie, tired and aching, suffered from depression that had been well earned, if circumstances earn you a bout of depression. She thought so. She told herself that she must be sub-normal since she was so tired, sad and weak all the time. Her self-esteem was in shambles and the cause of her depression. Her husband also yelled at her failures to keep the house to his expectations. Why couldn't she get a decent job? And she believed that she couldn't. It was all her fault; she wasn't any good, she emotionally reasoned.

It had taken ten years of not believing in herself and letting herself become his occasional door mat when at last she found out what it was that had destroyed her: her internal agreements to his verbal broadsides and the condemna-

tions of others that were supposedly designed by their authors to help her! She had never shown confidence in herself to him — or to others, for that matter.

With an all-out reversal she broke through her self-denigration, showed him her new confident self and, believing in God's love for her, found a respectful husband and personal liberation in just six weeks.

It may take longer or even fewer days for you since conditions will be different and your determined drive to be accepted and loved a matter for your own spirit.

Therefore, read the rest of this chapter and determine how much effort you will commit to the task. Decide on its value to you. Consider how effective you want your partnership with God to become.

The following method entails two initial days of mental and emotional orientation and then whatever time period, determined by your commitment, it takes you to complete to your satisfaction the mental rebuilding of your self-image. To build a strong self-image using this method takes, on the average, about 40 days if you work at it consistently. Forty days is an acceptable time frame for mental change. **The first two days will require the most time out of your day — about an hour or two. The rest of the 40 days will take constant repetition of our positive faith-**

filled affirmations (beliefs) about us and God, to-gether with a life that acts out these beliefs.

Once you have built a self-image that consistently acts out to others what God thinks of you, continue growing, using the same method, adding your wants from the first list to your daily affirmations and actions.

We will be using tried and true principles, all of which are found in the teachings of the Bible, for a renewed mind so that we can effectively change our beliefs about ourselves.

Please understand that this is not the only method to build your self-image. There are many successful ways, but this is the one I like best and the one with which I have had most success in helping others. It is consistent with the Bible and its teachings, and it partners with God so that we can become spiritual giants.

The Path to Positive Internal Power

(A method to positively change your self-image and simultaneously increase your faith in God)

We begin by simply identifying the changes we know we need to make.

DAY NUMBER ONE

1. ***List Number One:*** Make a list of the beliefs about your persona (self) you wish to change. We'll call it "List Number One" for ease of reference.

   A. When making this list it is imperative that you aim for a bull's eye not for a general area you want to improve. **Focus** is the name of success when trying to accomplish anything. So ask, what are the ***specific things*** I need to change or would like to change? It may be things like, "I hate myself," or, "I feel scared every time I face a new opportunity," or, "I need more confidence in talking to people."

   B. Once you have identified your list of desired changes, rewrite this list in the positive. "I wish to become a more confident person." "I want to be unafraid of change and new things." Never leave it in the negative. The negative is what you want to leave behind. The negative is looking back at what you want to change. The positive is looking forward to what you want to be. Don't look back if you want to make a positive change. *"Forgetting those things which are be-*

23

hind, I press toward the mark," Philippians 3:13, is Paul's advice taken from his own experience.

C. This list does not have to be complete because you are going to change one thing at a time and focus on one thing at a time. You will also add other goals in the future.

D. After you have successfully changed your self-image to be the same as God thinks about you, you will find other things (perhaps those you listed in this list, list number one) correcting themselves almost automatically.

E. You may need to extend this list later as other items emerge and you become aware of the need to change them.

THE PATH TO POSITIVE INTERNAL POWER
Calendar and worksheet

DAY ONE:
List Number One
Make a list of the beliefs about your persona (self) you wish to change. Write them below in the positive.

    <u>Example:</u> I wish to become a more confident person.

1. _____
2. _____
3. _____
4. _____
5. _____

24

Now we will begin the process of changing our self-image. We are first going to make a change in our attitude toward ourselves. To do this, make a second list. We will call this "List Number Two." (Creative, don't you think?) List all the good things you believe about yourself that you can recall. This list is not to show to others, so don't be shy or hesitant at recording ALL, even the little things that you can call "good." If you say, "I can't think of any," you are being negative and untruthful. You will need to be honest. No person is so bad they don't have a few good things about them. You must do a thorough job of this.

    A. You may list items such as:

            I am a kind person

            I care about my family

            I am a hard worker

            I say thank you most of the time

            I love God and try to love my neighbors.

    B. The idea about this list (list number two) is to be honest and to say it just like you see it and feel it about yourself.

    C. Note this also: **Whatever you believe, you must be willing to act out to others — all the other people you meet each day. I mean you must behave as though you really believe this and present yourself to others like you believe the things in this list. If you are not willing to act according to what you have written, you simply don't really believe it. Rephrase it until you can believe it and will**

25

act accordingly. It must be what you can believe and what you are, therefore, willing to act out to others. Now you have the instruction for your second list and first affirmation.

D. After you have made the list you will write an affirmation below the list. An affirmation is a phrase you are going to read and say to yourself daily until you have made a complete change of belief. Affirmations are simply talking to ourselves in order to change or confirm our beliefs about ourselves. We pay most attention to what we say to ourselves, not to what others say to us (including God – although this should not be so). Technically this is called psycholinguistics (soul language). More than anything else, this is what changes our beliefs provided what we are saying to ourselves is something that we believe. It's all about our beliefs and how to change them. Note: affirmations are not just saying empty words. They are not foolish internal murmurings. They define what you feel you can believe and they drill that positive belief into your conscious and subconscious mind. This is an affirmation you will keep changing, raising the bar as you climb toward believing God's beliefs about you. You are repairing the damage of years and that takes a very deliberate self-disciplined effort. You can do it. It's not climbing Mt. Everest in one leap!

E. Here's how to write your affirmation. Coin a phrase that sums up list number two — a phrase like, "I'm not so bad; I think I have some good in me." The more positive this affirmation is, the better. It could even be as positive as, "I am very good!" Keep reading before you decide how positive you can be.

F. However, remember, what you affirm MUST be something you can and do believe about yourself! Keep trimming it down to size if you can't believe what you have written and don't think you can live it out to others. Be very honest about what you can believe! It will be what you **can** believe about yourself that will make all the difference. So you must believe something positive — anything positive; anything, even if it is very small. That is called starting where you are. If you don't start at your present belief level it won't work. Starting small is no handicap!

G. Get that pencil moving!

THE PATH TO POSITIVE INTERNAL POWER
Calendar and worksheet

List Number Two: Make a list of all the good things you believe about yourself.

Example: I am a kind person

1. _____
2. _____
3. _____
4. _____
5. _____
6. _____
7. _____
8. _____
9. _____
10. _____

Affirmation for List Number Two:

Don't forget to add "I really believe this!" at the end of the affirmation the words.

_____
_____
_____
_____
_____
_____

Act out your belief to others all day long.

DAY TWO

<u>List Number Three:</u> Next make a list (List Number Three) of the good things God thinks and believes about you. (If you don't believe in God you should use some other method to build your self image.) List things like: When He created us He said we were "very good"; He wouldn't send His son to die for a worthless creature, would He? He loves me and, since that must take up some energy on His part, I must be good or He wouldn't waste His effort. Remember this also, He is planning to spend eternity with you — wow! If you do believe in God - truly that is — *you will begin to accept His evaluation of you* and that will make it so much easier to change your belief about yourself and raise the bar.

Write your second affirmation under this list, something like this, "God believes in me and thinks I am worth His every effort to transform me into His powerful and wonderful image!" Or, simply, "God believes I am very, very good!" Don't underestimate God's evaluation, now! When you repeat it to yourself put a big emphasis on VERY GOOD! You are listening to yourself, remember. Here's your worksheet. Go ahead and write.

THE PATH TO POSITIVE INTERNAL POWER
Calendar and worksheet

List Number Three: Make a list of the good things God thinks about you.

1. _____
2. _____
3. _____
4. _____
5. _____
6. _____
7. _____
8. _____
9. _____
etc.

Affirmation For List Number Three.
Don't forget to add the words "I really believe this!" at the end of your affirmation.

_____

_____

_____

_____

DAY 2 TO DAY 40

A. Read lists two and three and their affirmations over carefully and thoughtfully before going to bed on night two.

B. Repeat both affirmations to yourself many times on day two and say to yourself each time, "I believe this, I really do!" Remember, it's all about what you believe! I am asking you to say this affirmation that you already say you believe so that when you try to live by it you will discover whether you really believe it. If you do find you can live it consistently then start raising the bar (believing better about yourself) immediately. Re-write your affirmation to List Number Two.

C. This affirmation of what God believes about you is an ongoing affirmation that will become part of your conscious life from now till you die — that is, if you choose to be the best you can be. Keep reciting God's evaluation of you along with your own affirmation until the inconsistency between the two becomes very clear to you and you feel your faith in yourself being forced to the level of God's belief about you!

D. *Read both lists and their affirmations thoughtfully each day until you are consistently acting out your first affirmation to everyone.*

E. As each day passes you should become a little concerned about the difference between what you believe about yourself and what God believes about you. So, start raising the bar on what you believe about yourself. You will be aided to do this by what we call stretch — stretching a little to believe more about yourself. Now that you believe your affirmation and are consistent about acting it out, a small stretch is a manageable step. If you had writ-

31

ten: "I believe I am not so bad and I have some good points," try: "I believe I am good." Raise the bar on yourself! **Continue raising the bar as fast as your belief level will allow you.** Stop and go back if you find you can't believe your affirmation and act it out. If you are not acting out your belief to others it is for certain you do not believe it.

F. Watch the way the discrepancy between what you believe about yourself and God's evaluation of you niggles at the integrity of your faith in God and, therefore, helps you raise the affirmation on list number two. **These two things — stretch and challenging you to believe what God believes about you — are the effective motivations this method uses to help you raise your self-image.**

G. It doesn't matter how many days it takes. Keep raising the bar in the affirmation below List Number Two until it reads the same as what God believes about you!

ADD ITEMS FROM LIST NUMBER ONE

H. *When you have arrived at believing what God believes about you and living it out to others, start adding one specific item from list number one to your affirmation of what you believe about yourself.* Your affirmation could now read something like this, "I believe I am very good, just like God says, **and** I am also confident talking to others − I really believe this." Keep that added item in your affirmation until you can really say it is part of the way **you consistently present yourself to the outside world,** and then replace it with an-

32

other item from point one above. Do the same with it until you show this next item consistently to the world. You must not move on to another item from point one above until you are consistently showing your current affirmative belief to the world!

I. Use the principle of stretch to achieve this added belief. When you find a verse in the Bible that promises you what you are wanting, use that as your chief motivation. In the case above of wanting to be more confident when talking to others, it could be *"If God be for us who can be against us!"* The power of believing in God's promises to help your faith to change provides the ultimate drive.

J. **Add more items from List Number One as you are ready.** Keep improving your self-image and your public persona (your witness to God's power in you). Make both the inner and outer changes at the same time! Changing internally (your virtual world) without changing externally (your real world) is bound to fail after the dust has settled. Change both together. Your mind will be "putting on the mind of Christ." His faith and love and his positive internal power will start to be seen in your life, too. He wants this. Keep growing more and more like Jesus.

K. **Always, your faith in God will lift you faster than anything else — but not if your self-image is not improved along with your faith in God.** The disciples were timid and afraid after Jesus' death; but when the power of God's Spirit filled them at the event we call Pentecost they became very confident and bold! Their level of belief about themselves was directly affected by the feeling of the presence of God's Spirit in them. God was with

33

them and in them. They believed this. Your faith in God and your walk with God should also lift your self-image. Your spiritual life is directly linked to your self-concept. They rise and fall with each other. God made you "in His image" and as you become more like that image, you and everyone else will notice your spiritual growth. Your self-image and your belief in God are not two separate compartments in your life. I want to say it again; the one rises and falls with the other! There is no escaping this linkage. **Strengthen your faith in God and you will strengthen your self-esteem.** Paul linked both elements together when he said. *"I can do all things with Christ who strengthens me."* This is the truth about self-image and the truth about faith in God! Be careful of language that says, "It's God I believe in, not me." The Christian life is a partnership with God. Both are involved and we must rise with God and our faith in Him. I love strengthening people's faith in God for this reason. It's the greatest and fastest aid to an improved self-image if they will do both together.

THE PATH TO POSITIVE INTERNAL POWER
Calendar and worksheet

Each day is numbered so that you can record changes to your affirmation for List Number Two as you raise the bar.

Example: Progress from saying, "I think I am reasonably good," to saying, "I am very good," (see points 5-8). Please also record the addition of items from list number one (see points number 9-11) as you include them in your affirmation. This is your record of your progress.

3_____

4_____

5_____

6_____

8_____

9_____

10_____

11_____

12_____

13_____

14_____

15_____

16_____

17_____

18_____

19_____

20_____

21_____

22_____

23_____

24_____

25_____

26_____

27_____

28_____

29_____

30_____

31_____

32_____

33_____

34_____

35_____

36_____

37_____

38_____

39_____

40_____

Here is the formula in a matchbox.

*Formulate what you want to be.

*Ingrain what God thinks of you.

*With small steps believe more and more about yourself.

*Show each step to the world in the way you act and believe.

*Move on to the next item to be changed.

*Strengthen your faith in God and His power in you and you will transform your mind. (Romans 12:2)

Now you have it! It's so simple yet so few people exercise their faith and do it. If you haven't started, start today.

PART THREE

Helping Our Children to a Strong Self-Image

"Train up a child in the way he should go and when he is old he will not depart from it." (Proverbs 22:6)

Obviously a small child is not going to be able to understand all of the instructions for adults and be able to follow a detailed plan. No worries, mate (as they say down under).

Here is a path for parents to follow in helping develop their child's self-image.

1. ***Develop your own self-image.*** Children mimic their roll models. They are looking for models to learn from and they look to you. We don't learn in a vacuum we learn by finding a model and testing it. Observations have shown that, for children, the model their parents show them is the most important external factor in the development of their early self-images. And what they learn lasts! The self-image they learn to model in the first six years is the model for their life unless they consciously alter it. This is huge news to parents. A child's brain makes its greatest advance in the first six years of life. These are the formative years, I believe — even more so than teenage. Show them what you want them to be!

39

A. If they are older than six, don't say, "I'm too late." We are very adaptable, resilient creatures. God made us that way so that the limitations of time under which we live would not cause us a total loss when we make mistakes. Start anytime. Start now! Remember your children can consciously change what they have learned, just like you can. Model the changing of your self-image with them, letting them know what you are doing and letting them follow your progress if they are old enough to comprehend. Take them with you for the ride!

B. A disastrous practice of not influencing a child but letting them make their own choices in life is reaping its folly in society. Without positive models, a child will make uninformed choices and with limited wisdom, will often choose the self-damaging alternative. This popular theory of a decade or so ago for raising children fails to understand the limitations of the child and the child's dependence on adults to show it the right way to protect one's own self-concept.

2. Help them understand from the earliest age that positive thoughts about themselves are good and negative ones are bad. Help them identify the positive and the negative reactions they are having. Learn to do it yourself so they can see what it is all about. Teach them God is positive. Everything about Him is positive. Even when He corrects us He is being positive. Love, joy, and peace — the life of God - it's all positive. In fact, together with faith, these are the most potent, positive forces created by God and used by Him.

3. Fill their lives with lots of these "vitamins" to raise a healthy child. They learn self-discipline by being disciplined. Likewise they learn love and its positive powers by being loved and being taught to love. They learn self-love — you got it — by being loved.

4. Joy is essential for a growing healthy self-image. You are not responsible for their happiness. They are. So, breathe a sigh of relief. But you are responsible to do all you can to teach them how they can be happy and fulfilled.

   A. Doing what is right is one of the most important things for a child's (and for that matter an adult's) happiness. It avoids the ravages of guilt. That's one giant step to happiness. Teach them right and wrong.

   B. Loving God and others and loving themselves is obviously at the top of your list.

   C. Help them out of their sulky moods and their self-pity. By helping them I am saying to do everything you can to give them a helping hand. Scolding them out of a sulky mood seldom works. It is not harmful to offer them a treat if they will snap out of it and smile. Rewards are too under-rated among the skills of parenting. Distracting a little child is also an effective method early in their lives.

   D. Teach them. Parents are their main teachers. They identify with their home and their parents. Parents should take pains to teach them what a healthy attitude is and what an unhealthy attitude is. Healthy attitudes develop positive self-images.

   E. There are many other creative ways. Devise your own.

5. Peace is less understood. For a child, it is learning to live in harmony with others — learning the damage that war between siblings and parents can inflict, and the positive alternatives to strife. They will always, in the long run, do what is to their best advantage. So, teach them how to behave to their best advantage using methods that promote peace like forgiveness, kindness and giving the other person the benefit of the doubt. Show them that hurting others is not to their ultimate best advantage. Not only might they suffer the pains of successful revenge, but they destroy relationships and damage their own self-image. The good feeling they have when they get revenge is a false feeling. It will lead them further into trouble. Wrong is always wrong and has a deceptive face.

    A. Peace is also something you give someone when you let them win their own insignificant battle. Winning the war — not the skirmishes — of good and evil is far more important.

    B. It is also learning to appreciate the occasional quiet time, the relaxing moment. For some personalities and for some children this is a very short moment!

6. You must do their affirmations for them until they can do them for themselves. Do their affirmations by telling them that they are good. Tell them you appreciate them. Tell them God thinks they are very, very good. Feed back to them your pleasure and pride when they do good and kind things or achieve (without making achievement the end-all of life for a child). Don't tell them they are good when they have done wrong. They will not be able to differentiate between being good when they do good and when

they do wrong. Tell them that they have made a mistake that God is waiting to forgive. Teach them to ask God for forgiveness. Later, as they grow older, have them repeat affirmations <u>with you</u>. It is empowering to hear the voice of their father or mother saying the words of affirmation for them and with them. This emphasis on the positive will do wonders for their self-images and increase parent-child bonding. Talk to them about your affirmative self-talk.

7. Teach them to believe what God says. Show them your faith in God's promises! Use the Bible stories of faith to reinforce the example of your confidence in God. Don't ever be ashamed of your faith.

8. Help them understand their makeup. Show them why they do some things that reward them and other things that damage them. Their strengths reward them when used effectively and damage them when not used, or when miss-used, or when over-used. Show them!

9. Children will always behave according to what they feel on the inside. Know your child's temperament and guide them to rewarding feelings. The best way to know your child's temperament is to complete an InnerKinetics® Child Temperament Key. You can access the key at https://www.raywlincoln.com/.

10. With the help of a biblical life coach, determine their temperament and you will be greatly helped and amazed at the difference such knowledge of how God made them will change your home life and your parenting. A parent's influence in the life of a child is greatly increased if the child feels that they are being understood.

Joe and Melinda were at the end of their skills and their patience. Their seven year old son frequently burst into uncontrollable rages. His anger even scared his parents. By divine appointment (for nothing happens without God being in it) they heard about personality assessments. They spoke with a biblical life coach. Little Terrance's anger appeared to be a result of being hurt. The PA (Personality Assessment) confirmed it. He had little natural defense against the hurts that others deliberately or inadvertently flung at him and he reacted to hurt like we all do when we are wounded. They went home equipped with a 'tool'.

Next time he exploded his mother quickly went to him and gently said, "I know you are hurt. What can I do to make it better?" He melted in tears. She quoted the words of a similar temperament (Paul, the Apostle): "Be angry, but do not sin" (don't do the wrong thing). The child could be angry for being hurt but was soon learning to do the right thing, and a great healing home was being born. This is the kind of help you can get when you tailor the teaching to the child's temperament.

Within a week the home had been transformed and a little boy was experiencing a love he had not known and understanding that reached his tender heart. A new chapter of parental care had begun with a self-image on the heal.

Don't be afraid to get help and use the knowledge of how God made your child. It will most probably involve learning the feelings of someone very different from you.

Understand Your Child and How He/She Feels

Although the following words sound a little rough they have motivated many.

"Don't be like the horse or the mule without understanding." (Psalm 32:9)

Developing Your Child's Positive Internal Power
The Steps to Help Your Child

Children require that you understand how they feel. Most of the time they can't explain it to you or don't want to. Of course they assume you know.

The only way we have of approximating what they feel is to know their temperament. Since most parents aren't experts on temperament and assessing temperaments, the help of a biblical life coach makes all the difference. However, the first step you can take is to complete the InnerKinetics® Child Temperament Key mentioned early, which can be accessed at https://www.raywlincoln.com/.

The following is a summary of the main points made in the discussion above. Working on these will help build a healthy self-image into your child's belief pattern. As with adults, faith in God is of prime importance. God bless you as you proceed.

Steps to take:

1. Develop your own self-image. You can't help them if yours is low.
2. Model how you are changing your self-image for your children to follow. Take them with you for the ride.
3. Teach them right and wrong. Guilt devastates healthy self images.
4. Teach them the difference between positive and negative thoughts about themselves. Do this as occasion arises.
5. Teach them God is positive in all his thoughts and we should be, too.
6. Give them plenty of the "soul vitamins" — love, joy and peace. Give them plenty of love and teach them that to give love feels even better.
7. Teach them how to be happy. Here are some basic elements of happiness.
   A. Do what is right.
   B. Love God and others.
   C. Don't sulk. It doesn't do any good.
   D. Healthy attitudes make a happy mind.
8. Teach them that peace is better than strife. To seek peace is always to their best advantage.
   A. Teach them revenge only makes matters worse.
   B. Provide some quiet times (short ones).
9. Tell them how good they are. That's saying their affirmations for them. Do this daily.
10. Teach them to believe what God says; show them your faith in God's Word.
11. Help them understand how God has made them. You will need a personality assessment to do this.

12. Help them use their strengths correctly. Remember, God did not give us any weaknesses. We create our weaknesses when we don't use our strengths, or miss-use them, or over-use them. Show them how you use yours correctly.

PART FOUR

Helping Teenagers to Self-Image Power

Here's where parents have a challenge! Don't cop out! A cop-out becomes a drop-out. Parents are not supposed to be drop-outs!

Now that you have gathered your nerve let me sketch the road ahead.

Teenagers are renowned for knowing everything — not all teens, but a good number. The first hurdle you will have to overcome is convincing them of their need to make changes to their self-image. If your teenager realizes their need, you can be thankful.

1. Convincing a teenager of the need of self-image changes, and then instilling the desire can be helped by the following:

    A. Use a personality assessment to flag them of their strengths and show them how they can, by improving their self-images, be all that they can be. To do this you will need to get your teen (14 years of age or older) to complete the InnerKinetics® Adult Temperament Key (with your guidance, if necessary). You can access the key at https://www.raywlincoln.com/temperament-key/#/intro. Then, if possible, meet with a biblical InnerKinetics life coach and make a preliminary assessment of their personality type. Then, the coach can confirm or adjust these findings. Some teenagers will be able to take the assessment; but for most, unless they are late in their teens, much of what is asked requires an understanding of their preferences that comes from experience with themselves, of which as yet they have little. The best path can be discussed and chosen.

B. Paint the picture of what they can be and can become as opposed to what they could easily settle for.

Teens are oscillating between living it up and figuring it out; between experiencing the pleasure of life's offerings and finding out what they really are (why they are thinking and feeling the things they do) and what they must do to find the best life. This is not so much a rational search but a *feel* for where they should go. Therefore, painting them pictures of success and failure (there are many biblical examples) and presenting them with models and challenges stimulates them and feeds their quest for the knowledge of what life really is all about. Some personalities are bent toward the immediate gratification of life's experiences (SP's). Others are leaning toward the discovery of values to live by (SJ's and NF's). All will factor in the values they have learned. So paint the picture of values and worth. Challenge them to higher ground.

Peter (now in his 40's) looked back on his teenage and said:

"I was embarrassed by my looks and afraid of what that might mean for my future. I was confused about why different people lived by different standards. I had a very low self-image and lacked confidence and, of course, direction. My Dad did not have the time to spend with me; and I didn't want to live like he lived because he didn't seem to have the answers to my questions. The life he lived seemed to be a shallow life. Looking back I never knew what his values really were. I was introduced to a man who had time for me and seemed to know where he was going in life and had a clear set of values so I modeled after him. And that determined the course of my life! Thankfully, he was a follower of Jesus and had it all together. So, Jesus became my hero and I fought for Jesus and His values among my other teen friends."

Picture life and its true values and model them. It will build self-esteem in teens because a sense of knowing where you are going always does.

Teach them that God made them a certain way (the way their personality assessment reveals) and it is foolish not to know how you are made and why.

C. Arrange a small PA (personality assessment) party for friends (with their parent's approval) to assess their personality profile and have lots of fun doing it. (Beforehand, have the parents gather with a biblical life coach for a pre-assessment of their teenager's type to establish a basic probability.)

2. Once assessed take them through the steps for affirmations used for adults and help them with some of their choices. Explain the need to learn how to present themselves to the world of others — friends and all people.

3. Help them understand what is going on in their minds and the formation of their lives. *"As a man thinks, so is he."* *(Proverbs 23:7)*

4. Walk them through your affirmations (statements in the growth of your faith) and take them for the ride with you. Model the repairing of your self-image for them.

5. Encourage them to talk about what they want most to believe about themselves. Guide them in their designing of their steps toward a strong self-image. Use the method and worksheets taught in this book.

6. Have your youth group get involved in mass and thus make it a "cool thing." Use the exercise as a journey to strengthen their faith in themselves as well as strengthening their faith in God since the both must go together.

7. The different personality types will want some special attention in reaching their goals. They may need slightly different motivations and insights. Leaders and parents can easily be coached in these differences. This is not a must, but a help.

8. Make it a fun adventure. There is no end to creativity.

Conclusion

You can walk this journey of improving your self beliefs and those of your children alone or with another's help (a life-coach who uses biblical psychology).

If you are depressed, don't walk your journey alone! Please don't!

If your child is depressed (not uncommon), get the help you need in parenting a depressed child.

If you are confused about how to do some of this, don't travel alone. Use a biblical life coach. It makes sense doesn't it?

Since you really need a personality assessment to find out how God has made you and, therefore, how best to walk this path to power, you need to visit a biblical life coach to begin the journey of self-understanding with understanding how God has made you.

Worship, prayer, and utilizing the positive power of God's Word will make the path even faster since it will strengthen you and your faith in God. We all respond to following the way God made us to function. But those with a faith in God complete the making of a holistic, healthy and powerful creation. Faith alone is the way to salvation. Once having believed and found God's forgiveness and acceptance, get involved in working out your own salvation in your life (partnering with God), just as the Apostle Paul said.

My seminars on *Be All That You Can Be* and *A Life Full of Faith* could help you make a giant leap forward instead of a feeble step into the unknown.

God bless you and make you all you were intended by God to be!

ABOUT THE AUTHOR

Ray Lincoln has served as senior pastor to single and multi-staffed churches in New Zealand, Australia and the USA. His 40 years of experience in coaching, counseling and teaching have given him the opportunity to guide many people to self-discovery and spiritual renewal. He has studied extensively in the areas of Psychology, Theology, Philosophy and Personology.

Teaching people to succeed in life and overcome their challenges with God's strength are his passion. Ray says, "While remaining true to the teachings of the Bible, my strong interest has been to use the best of science and develop a true Biblical Psychology that can help people find true fulfillment. God wants this for all of us. He knows best how we function and has left us the most helpful life-manual in the best-selling book ever!"

Conducting well over one hundred seminars in Australia, New Zealand and the USA has led him to lecture in universities, seminaries, and Bible colleges as well as businesses and churches. He has mentored pastors and other professionals. Ray has a deep faith in God, strengthened by his studies, and offers his services, experience, and knowledge to you. His wife, Mary Jo, is more than a willing partner in his ministry and in her own right, contributes much to their joint mission.

Books by Ray W. Lincoln

If you prefer to read books that get right to the heart of the matter, you will find them in this list. The goal in producing these monographs is to provide immediate help in an easy-to-read and quick-to-assimilate format. The topics were chosen from help most often sought by Dr. Lincoln's clients, friends, and church members where he was pastor. More books are on the way! So stay in touch!

The Art of Encouragement – Everyone needs encouragement so more encouragers are needed. Do you long to be an encourager to your loved one or friend who is hurting, grieved or depressed? Learn the basic skills in this helpful guide. **$6.95**

Finding God's Will for You – How can I know what God wants me to do and be? Ray Lincoln has been asked this question countless times over his forty plus years of ministry. Here he guides his readers through fundamental steps to determining God's will and obtaining the peace of confident faith. **$6.95**

"I love you," signed Jesus – The inspiring account of Christ's suffering as you have not heard it told before. First printed in New Zealand and "sold out," this scholarly study into the details of Christ's passion will stir you to love and serve the One who died that we might live. **$6.95**

COMING SOON

How God Handles Depression – Using the deep depression of Elijah, Dr. Lincoln uncovers the surprising way God treats depression and nurtures us back to health and happiness.

Willed in Heaven and Made to Work on Earth – What is the secret to a long and happy marriage? In this monograph is revealed the "real secret" that is really no secret at all. Using the example of the marriage of Mary and Joseph, which had all the elements to create failure, the author shows how God designed the marriage relationship to work.

Personal Excellence – Eleven principles to adopt from the life of Christ that will guide you to success in all your endeavors.

www.raywlincoln.com
www.innerkinetics.com

www.ingramcontent.com/pod-product-compliance
Lightning Source LLC
Chambersburg PA
CBHW060714030426
42337CB00017B/2869